Federal Protectors

NSA

BARBARA LOWELL

BLACK RABBIT BOOKS

Bolt is published by Black Rabbit Books
P.O. Box 227, Mankato, Minnesota 56002
www.blackrabbitbooks.com

Alissa Thielges, editor; Michael Sellner, designer
and photo researcher

Library of Congress Cataloging-in-Publication Data
Names: Lowell, Barbara, author.
Title: NSA / by Barbara Lowell.
Other titles: National Security Agency
Description: Mankato, Minnesota: Black Rabbit Books, [2024] |
Series: Federal protectors | Includes bibliographical references and index. |
Audience: Ages 8-12 | Audience: Grades 4-6 |
Summary: "Breaking secret codes and listening in on enemy meetings are just the beginning of what members of the NSA do. Find out what NSA agents do to keep the United States safe"—Provided by publisher.
Identifiers: LCCN 2022024143 (print) | LCCN 2022024144 (ebook) |
ISBN 9781623106195 (library binding) | ISBN 9781623106256 (ebook)
Subjects: LCSH: United States. National Security Agency—History—Juvenile literature. | Intelligence service—United States—Juvenile literature.
Classification: LCC UB256.U6 L69 2024 (print) | LCC UB256.U6 (ebook) |
DDC 327.1273009—dc23/eng/20220524
LC record available at https://lccn.loc.gov/2022024143
LC ebook record available at https://lccn.loc.gov/2022024144

Printed in China

Image Credits

123RF/peshkov 10–11; Alamy/Jonathan ORourke 18 (t), Pictorial Press Ltd 6; Crypto Museum Foundation/Crypto Museum 19 (all); Dreamstime/Greg Randles 13 (tr), Moreno Soppelsa 22, 23 (b); European Pressphoto Agency/Jim Lo Scalzo 13 (br); Getty/Getty Images Staff 4–5, Saul Loeb 12–13 (bkgd); iStock/dima_zel 20 (b), EvgeniyShkolenko 15, Fertnig 12 (r), gorodenkoff 28–29, LaylaBird 25, monsitj 16; NSA/CSS/Sky News 12 (l); Shutterstock/19srb81 27, BEST-BACKGROUNDS 3, 26–27 (bkgd), Gorodenkoff cover, 9, imagestockdesign 6–7, Neo Edmund 1, 31, NewSaetiew 18–19 (bkgd), NotarYES 23 (t), Vector Tradition 9 (bkgd), Wawx 32; U.S. Army/Watervliet Arsenal Public Affairs 20 (t); U.S. Navy/Petty Officer 1st Class Pedro Rodriguez 13 (l); U.S.D.O.D./Ron Stern 20 (mid); Wikimedia Commons/Public Domain 18 (b)

CONTENTS

CHAPTER 1

Finding BIN LADEN

Osama bin Laden was a **terrorist**. He was America's number one enemy. The United States searched for him. The National Security Agency (NSA) helped. They listened to his phone calls. They found information on him. They searched for almost ten years.

Pakistan

The Catch

In 2011, they finally caught him. The NSA found his hiding place. U.S. Navy Seals flew to Pakistan. They stormed his house and killed him. Finding enemies and their plans are important jobs for the NSA.

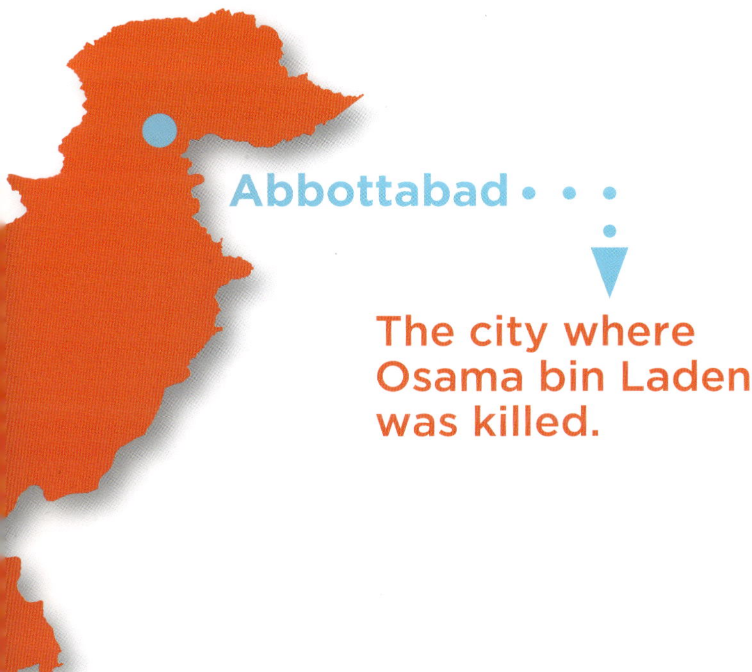

CHAPTER 2

Top SECRET

The NSA is a U.S. **intelligence agency**. It gathers information from **foreign** places. It breaks coded messages. It spies on enemies. Are they getting ready to attack? The NSA finds out. It learns their plans. The NSA also works to keep America's secrets safe.

The White House receives threat reports from the NSA within ten minutes.

NSA Collects Information From:

phone calls

emails

text messages

online chats

social media

photos

videos

Facing Danger

America faces danger from around the world. Enemies plan attacks. They use the Internet to spread lies. They try to steal U.S. **data** and property. The NSA finds and studies enemies' data. It warns U.S. leaders about any danger.

PROTECTING NSA HEADQUARTERS

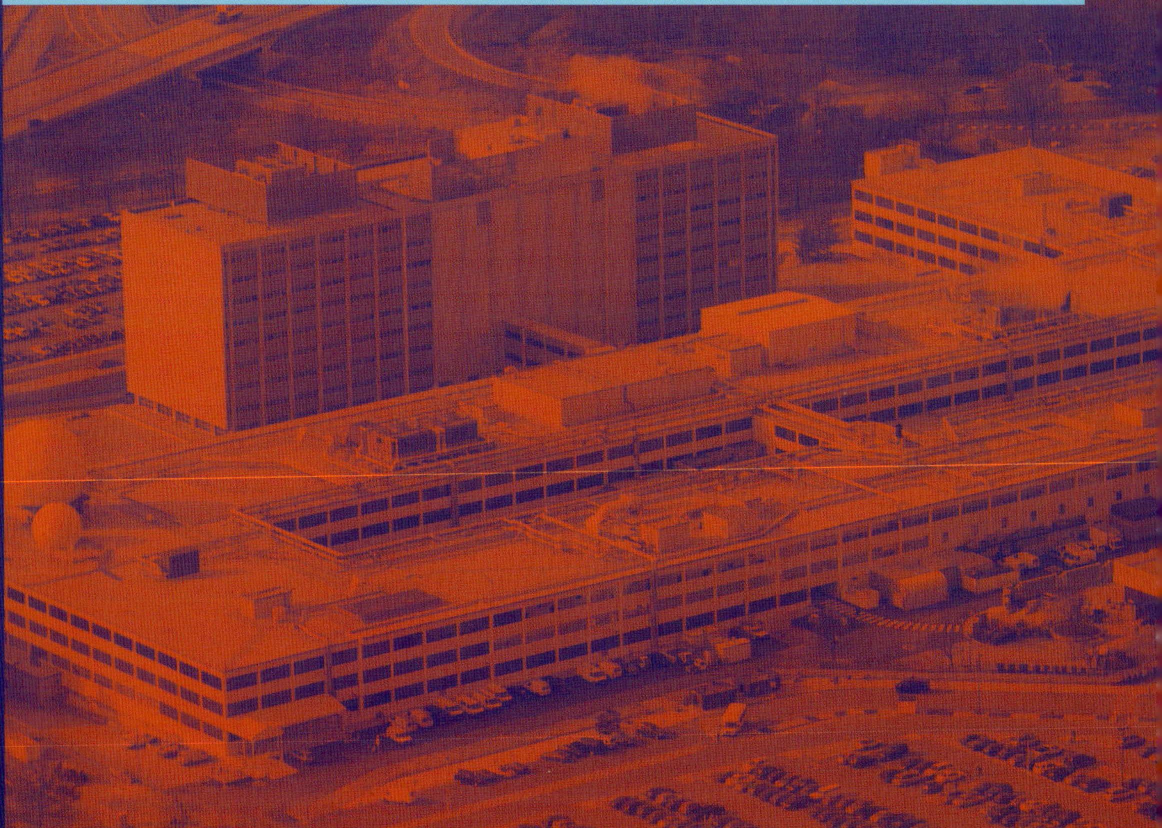

BARRIERS

BOMB-SNIFFING DOGS

RAZOR WIRE

WARNING SIGNS

NSA POLICE

CHAPTER 3

Breaking CODES

America's enemies send messages in **code**. Codes are like puzzles. The NSA works to break those codes. The people who do this work are called **cryptologists**. The NSA has the best code-crackers in the country. They learn if terrorists are planning attacks. They find who is giving our enemies money. The NSA stops attacks that would harm U.S. computers.

A nickname for the NSA is "Puzzle Palace."

mirror_mod.mirror_object
operation == "MIRROR_X":
mirror_mod.use_x = True
mirror_mod.use_y = False
mirror_mod.use_z = False
operation == "MIRROR_Y":
mirror_mod.use_x = False
mirror_mod.use_y = True
mirror_mod.use_z = False
operation == "MIRROR_Z":
mirror_mod.use_x = False
mirror_mod.use_y = False
mirror_mod.use_z = True
election at the end -add
_ob.select= 1
er_ob.select=1
ntext.scene.objects.activ
("Selected" + str(modifie
irror_ob.select = 0
bpy.context.selected_ob
ata.objects[one.name].se
int("please select exactl
OPERATOR CLASSES
NODE 04
NODE 05
NODE 02
NODE 06
BLOCK 01
NODE 03
BLOCK 01
NODE 01
NATIONAL SECU
UNITED STA

Creating Codes

The NSA creates codes too. Many are math problems that are difficult to master. The codes are hard to break. This blocks enemies from understanding our messages. American secrets stay safe.

NSA ENCRYPTION HISTORY

The NSA uses machines to keep secrets safe. They have gotten better over the years. You need an encryption key to use them.

1950–1970s

Typewriters with a spinning rotor that encrypted text; messages delivered by hand

1960–1980s

Large, electronic machines with vacuum tubes; used a punched card as a key

1980s

Machines with a computer chip; smaller, faster, and could be used in the field

1990-2000s

Keys with chips that are updated electronically and plugged into phones

2000-today

Machines protect data sent over the Internet

on land

under the sea

in outer space

Working with the Military

The U.S. military works around the world. It guards and defends our country. NSA members work with the military. They uncover the enemy's plans. They give soldiers safe ways to communicate. The NSA creates codes to keep U.S. weapons systems safe.

Where the NSA Protects

Military Communication

Recycling Secrets

The NSA uses advanced computer systems for codes. But it still shares secrets on printed paper. When the papers are no longer needed, the NSA destroys them. The NSA has its own recycling plant. The papers mix with water and heat. They turn into **pulp** that is used to make new paper.

RECYCLING Process

paper shredding

paper pulp

new paper

CHAPTER 4

Working for the NSA

The NSA looks for people with math and computer skills. They need people who speak foreign languages. The NSA offers a three-year training program to new employees. Classes cover languages, math, computer science, gathering data, and other subjects.

The NSA offers a work-study program to high school seniors.

NSA By the Numbers

65,000 CUBIC FEET OF SECRET PAPERS KEPT ON FILE

17 types of jobs at the NSA

130 languages the NSA listens to

70,000

visitors to the National Cryptologic Museum each year

16 number of U.S. agencies receiving NSA's intelligence information

TOP SECRET number of people working for the NSA

Keeping America Safe

The NSA works hard to keep America safe. It breaks and creates codes 24/7. It listens to foreign conversations. It gathers enemy's information. It prevents terrorist attacks. The NSA works behind the scenes to keep America safe every day.

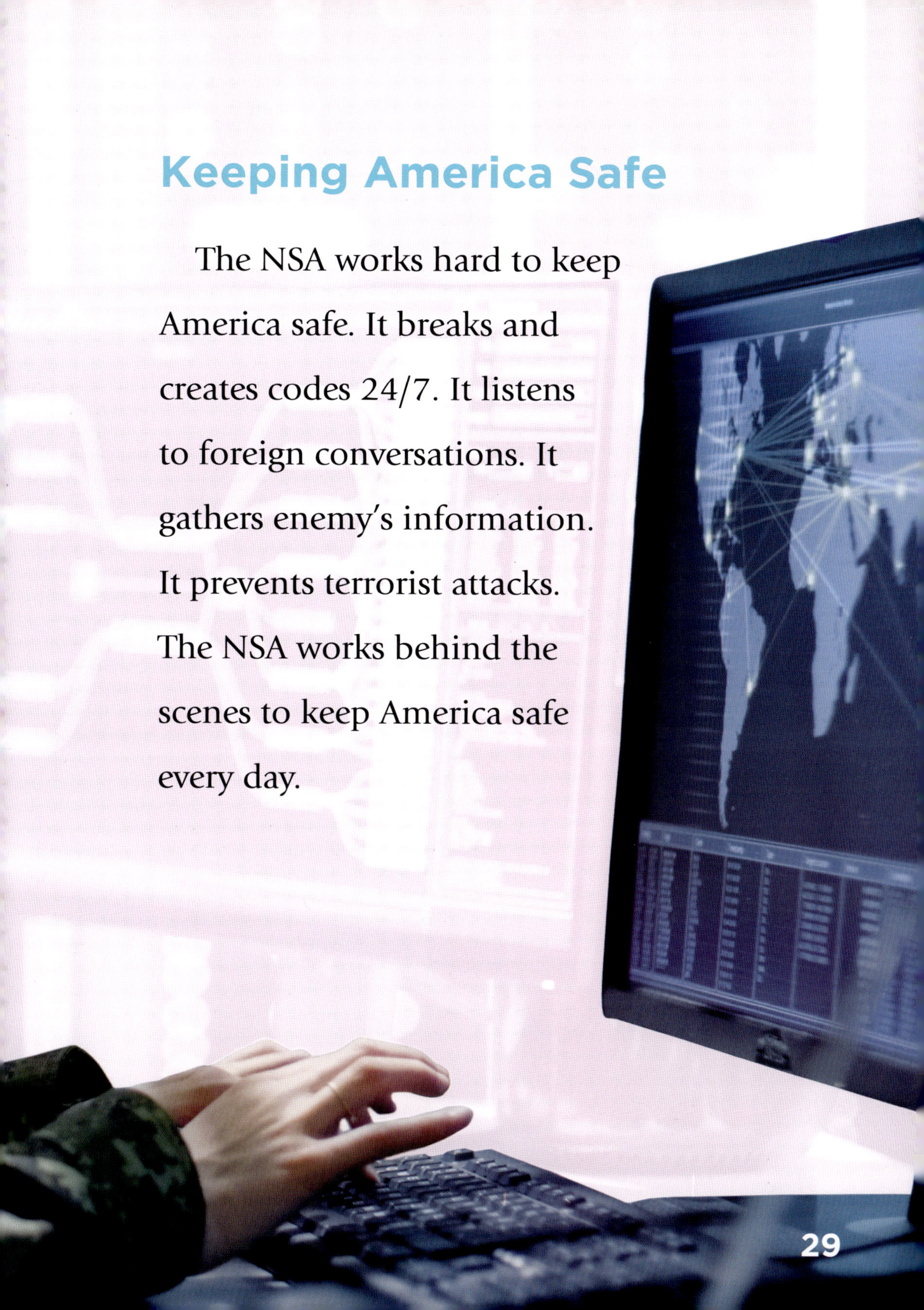

code (KOHD)—a set of letters, numbers, symbols, etc., used to secretly send messages

cryptologist (krip-TOL-uh-jist)—a person who studies codes and can translate coded messages

data (DAT-uh)—information created or stored by a computer

encryption (en-KRIP-shun)—the process of changing information into a code

foreign (FAWR-in)—located outside your own country

intelligence agency (in-TEL-i-juhns AY-juhn-see)—a government department that collects military or political information

pulp (PUHLP)— a soft, wet material made of water and paper

terrorist (TER-or-ist)—someone who uses violence or threats to frighten people into obeying

BOOKS

Daigneau, Jean. *Code Cracking for Kids.* Chicago: Chicago Review Press, 2020.

Thomas, Rachael L. *Professional Cryptologists.* Minneapolis: Lerner Publications, 2022.

Townsend, Chris. *Inside the NSA.* New York: Enslow Publishing, 2019.

WEBSITES

About NSA/CSS
www.nsa.gov/about/

Nat Geo Kids: Crack the Code Game
kids.nationalgeographic.com/games/action-adventure/article/crack-the-code-1

Virtual STEM for Kids: Codes and Ciphers
nsufl.libguides.com/virtual-stem/codes-ciphers

INDEX